25 Totally Terrific Social Studies Activities

Step-by-Step Directions for Motivating Projects That Students Can Do Independently

Kathy Pike, Jean Mumper & Paula Beardell Krieg

New York • Toronto • London • Auckland • Sydney
Mexico City • New Delhi • Hong Kong • Buenos Aires

Teaching Resources

Dedication

To our husbands and best friends, who
encourage us with every stroke of the pen:
Tom Pike—K.P.
Robert Mumper—J.M.

To Becky Potter for her caring, wisdom,
and support—P.B.K.

Editor: Mela Ottaiano
Cover and interior design: Maria Lilja
ISBN-13: 978-0-439-49830-2
ISBN-10: 0-439-49830-9

1 2 3 4 5 6 7 8 9 10   40   15 14 13 12 11 10 09

Contents

Introduction

Exploring Hands-On Projects in Social Studies

Exploring new possibilities! Much of the content and learning in social studies is the result of the work of innovative, creative individuals who have looked for better solutions to problems and more effective ways to better the quality of life. This book was designed to likewise explore new possibilities and perhaps make its contribution to the social studies curriculum by providing alternate ways to assess student learning using activities that go beyond traditional reports and tests, and engaging ways to showcase student learning.

Social studies embodies a wide range of disciplines and learning—in history, geography, civics, and economics—and calls upon the use of many skills, such as map reading, note taking, reading charts and graphs, and analyzing primary source

ABC Famous Places to Visit in the USA

Compiled by Mrs. Mumper's Fifth Grade '96

documents. Much of the learning in the past has typically revolved around the use of a single textbook, and assessment has consisted of tests and reports. More recently, however, teaching social studies means providing opportunities for students to learn not only from the textbook, but also from primary sources, trade books, maps, journals, newspapers, the Internet, video clips, and so on. This approach has enriched the social studies curriculum, making it more meaningful and purposeful for the learner. The activities in this book also aim to enrich the curriculum, extending the ways students can present what they have learned.

To boost the quality and accuracy of information in the finished projects, we begin the activities with some effective research strategies, such as I-Charts and two-column note taking, to encourage students to use multiple sources for locating key information, ask relevant questions, and determine appropriate content. We also provide some assessment measures, a rubric (page 14) and a self-evaluation form (page 13), which point out the qualities for producing exemplary products and give students an opportunity to self-reflect and monitor their learning and efforts.

The majority of this book is devoted to the projects themselves. There are 25 to choose from, with some added variations. Many of the formats can be used interchangeably for the same content. For example, both graduated-pages books and folded-circle books lend themselves to geographical studies of states, countries, and continents. This flexibility allows for class variation in presenting the same topic. The graduated-pages format also works well for presenting biographies, state facts, colonial life, inventions, the life of a Civil War soldier, and more.

Keep in mind that the ideas presented in this book are intended as models and sources of inspiration. You are sure to come up with many more ideas of your own. Since exploration is essential to a social studies curriculum, now is the time for you to explore the possibilities that can extend the learning that is occurring in your classroom.

Enjoy the journey!
Kathy, Jean, and Paula

Mapping Out the Activities

Each project follows a predictable pattern by including a description of the project, additional social studies project ideas, a literature connection, clear directions for constructing the project, and an image of the finished project.

The hands-on activities in this book are based on simplicity. It's possible for students to create impressive finished projects with supplies you have on hand right now.

Supplies

Paper: Regular 8½" x 11" copy paper is well suited for most of the projects in this book. Colored papers, used at your discretion, can help dress up a project. Occasionally, some of the projects call for heavier weight paper (such as 65 pound), which is available at most office supply stores.

Keys to Success

For the best results, keep in mind a few key things:

- A project should require a minimum amount of preparation time on your part.

- Project supplies should be easily available and relatively inexpensive.

- Be sure students know how to fold, cut, and glue correctly.

- Giving one very clear instruction at a time (and allowing students to work slowly) will ultimately help the project go more quickly and more successfully.

- It's helpful to show a well-done example of what students will be making before the lesson begins.

Scissors: Students should have access to scissors that really work. Try out the scissors in your classroom—if you can't cut with them, neither can students. If scissors are in short supply and you can't readily obtain more, teach students how to make sharp folds, then tear along the fold. (You may also do the cutting for them or have them create projects that don't require cutting.)

Glue: Most of the projects call for glue. We recommend using glue sticks. There are lots of very bad glue sticks on the market, which can really sabotage a project, so look for UHU glue sticks. Buying them by the dozen in a large size is the most economical way to go. If you don't have access to decent glue sticks, use whatever works for you, be it judicious use of white glue, staples, lacing, taping, or whatever it is you discover to be the most functional and manageable.

Colored pencils: When adding illustrations to the projects, neatness counts. Colored pencils work the best. If you don't have them, crayons are the next best choice, followed by colored markers. Markers tend to give a messy look unless used carefully. If you and students prefer markers, try those with a fine tip.

Rubber bands: Some of the projects call for using this quick, no mess, inexpensive, fun-to-use fastener. (Just be sure to hand them out one at a time!) Try to have different sizes on hand, in particular, #19, #16, and #33.

Other materials: A handful of projects call for some other readily available supplies, such as file folders, craft sticks, boxes, and resealable plastic bags.

Review the Essential Steps

Never take it for granted that students somewhere, somehow, have acquired the skills to fold, cut, and glue. Here are some suggestions to help with this:

Folding: When folding a piece of paper in half, share the "capture" tip with students. Students hold the matching corners firmly, once they have lined them up. Then starting at the edge of the paper that is placed flat on the desk, keeping the paper captured with one hand, use a finger of the other hand to slide across the paper toward the part that will be folded. Finish the fold by sliding the finger up and down the folded edge.

Cutting: If the scissors are of a high quality and students are still having trouble cutting, watch to see what part of the scissors they are using to make the cut. Opening the scissors wide enough to cut with the back part of the blade works the best. Students should not try to cut with the tip of the scissors. Some students will cut better making a series of micro cuts. Others will cut well if they make a series of long cuts. If necessary, discretely sit a student having too much difficulty next to a helpfully minded, skilled cutter who can assist.

Gluing: Any project can come unglued, even with the best glue sticks, if proper care is not taken. When gluing two objects together, press them together firmly so that they will stay stuck together once the glue dries. Then put the project under something heavy, such as a book, until the glue dries completely.

Instruction

It may be tempting to demonstrate the first several steps in the sequence of a project, however, when it's time for students to begin, it is best to give just one direction at a time. While you show each step, students can do it along with you. By staying together, everyone can be successful.

It's also helpful to provide both visual and spoken instructions for each step. You may even want to create a handout from the illustrations provided in the book to show the sequence of steps.

Be sure you all agree on certain necessary terms. For example, when you want students to fold their paper in half, long edge to long edge, ask students to fold their paper using the "hot dog fold," which results in a folded paper that looks long and narrow. When you want students to fold the paper in half, short edge to short edge, ask the students to fold their paper "book fold," so that the proportions of the paper are suggestive of a book. (See illustrations, at right.)

Hot Dog Fold

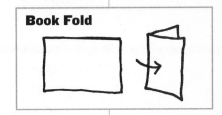

Book Fold

Sample project: Before you start any project, it's a good idea to show students what the finished project could look like. Turn to the photographs in this book or make a prototype yourself to share.

Project content: Students may create visually interesting projects, but the end product will only be as good as its contents. If students do not know how to conduct research or write up their findings, their reports can mirror encyclopedia articles. Since no one wants to read report after report that resembles a mini-encyclopedia, nonfiction writing should be a significant and ongoing instructional goal. Specifically related to these projects, assign or guide students in choosing a topic worth investigating and encourage them to research it using multiple sources. After students have obtained enough data and information to develop their topics adequately, they should organize the content and present it in such a manner that it is readable and engaging. If students have ample opportunity to read quality nonfiction texts, they will become familiar with the elements that make books or articles effective and interesting, and transfer what they have learned to their own writing.

Professional Resources

Buehl, D. (2001). *Classroom Strategies for interactive learning.* Newark, DE: International Reading Association.

Pike, K. & Mumper, J. (1998). *Books don't have to be flat.* New York: Scholastic.

Pike, K., Mumper, J., & Fiske, A. (2003). *Quick quilts across the curriculum.* New York: Scholastic.

Wood, K. (2001). *Literacy strategies across the subject areas.* Boston: Allyn & Bacon.

Research Strategies

Without other strategies in place, students frequently use only a single source in their research. They may simply go to an encyclopedia or the Internet, locate their topics, and copy entire text. With the latter, in particular, students typically don't check to verify the authenticity or the usefulness of the information they find. To assist students in their research and to ensure that they use multiple sources, there are several excellent strategies they can utilize. Two of them are presented here: I-Charts and Two-Column Notes (Buehl, 2001; Wood, 2001).

Inquiry or I-Charts

I-Charts are matrixes for helping students generate meaningful inquiry questions for their investigations using multiple sources. They assist students in researching their questions and organizing their information. The topic of the investigation is written on the top of the page. Right below the title are boxes for recording the interesting facts, figures, and information students find. The sources for this inquiry are listed along the side of the chart (for example, the Internet, trade books, news magazines, newspapers, textbooks, primary source documents), along with a space for writing in previously known information ("What I Already Know"). At the bottom of the chart is space for summarizing the data and for recording any new questions. (See example, below left.)

Two-Column Notes

This research strategy, also known as a Double-Entry Journal, is designed to assist students in processing and reflecting on information that they read or learn. It is a system of note taking where students engage in a discussion with the author, responding to, reflecting on, or questioning information that was read. All that is needed for this activity is a piece of paper divided into two sections (T-Charts also work well). In the left-hand column, students record information from the text. They write their comments in the right-hand column. There are many variations of this strategy, depending on the headings or prompts you provide. (See example, below right.)

Possible Prompts for Two-Column Notes

Information From the Book	My Response to the Information
What I Already Know About the Topic	Questions I Have About the Topic
What I Know About the Topic	What I Learned About the Topic
What Is Significant Information	What Is Interesting Information
Facts I Read	Questions I Still Have
Opinions in the Text	Evidence or Proven Facts
Quotes in the Text	My Reactions to the Quotes

Student _Taylor_   Date _11/06_

I-Chart

Topic Inventions	Guiding Questions			Other interesting information:
	1. How are inventions made ?	2. Who are some famous inventors ?	3. How have inventions changed our world ?	
What I Already Know	New inventions are made every day.	Thomas Edison invented light bulbs.		
Source 1 * Computer * Compton's Encyclopedia	Ben Franklin did experiments with electricity and a kite.	Ben Franklin invented more than 50 things.	The Franklin stove was able to heat a whole house.	
Source 2 * Interview: Mr. Walsh	Mr. Walsh wanted to make his job easier.	Mr. Walsh made a wood splitter for logs.	He was 59 when he made his invention.	
Source 3 Trade book: Inventors by Martin Sandler		Thomas Edison Wright Brothers Isaac Singer	communication electricity flying/airplanes sewing machine	
Summary Inventions change the way we live. Now we can communicate on telephones and computers. Now we can fly to far away places in one day. we can sew clothes in one hour instead of doing it by hand. We can split wood for a whole winter in one week. Inventions make life easier.				**New questions?** What is a patent?

25 Totally Terrific Social Studies Activities © 2009 by Kathy Pike, Jean Mumper & Paula Beardell Krieg, Scholastic Inc. • page 10

Student _Janelle_   Date _3/21_

Two-Column Notes

Topic _____ The Grand Canyon

What I Already Know About the Topic	Questions I Have About the Topic
The Grand Canyon is very deep.	What is the deepest point? How long does it take to hike there?
Rattle snakes, coyote, and mountain lions live there.	What other animals are native to the Grand Canyon?
The Colorado River runs through the Grand Canyon.	Where does the Colorado River begin and end?
Many tourists visit the Grand Canyon each year.	How many tourists visit annually and what are the top five activities they do there?
The temperature can be very warm during the day and cold during the night.	What are the average monthly high and low temperatures? Is it considered an arid climate?

25 Totally Terrific Social Studies Activities © 2009 by Kathy Pike, Jean Mumper & Paula Beardell Krieg, Scholastic Inc. • page 11

Student _____ Date_____

I-Chart

Topic	Guiding Questions			Other interesting information:
	1. _____ _____ _____ _____ ?	2. _____ _____ _____ _____ ?	3. _____ _____ _____ _____ ?	
What I Already Know				
Source 1				
Source 2				
Source 3				
Summary				New questions?

Student _____ Date_____

Two-Column Notes

Topic _____

Evaluation/Rubrics

In order to be effective, assessment in social studies, as in any content area, must contain a variety of measures that include reports, tests, projects, self-evaluation, teacher observation, anecdotal records, and so forth. This book provides a means of showcasing and assessing student learning in social studies. In undertaking these projects as both an instructional and assessment tool, remember to consider these aspects: the content, the activity itself, and the final product. A beautifully crafted project without relevant and accurate content is useless for transmitting what has been learned or researched. On the other hand, accurate information that is sloppily presented probably will not be read by its intended audience.

The assessment measures suggested in this book include the following:

Self-evaluation: The benefits for self-evaluation are many, as it encourages student responsibility for their own learning and facilitates self-reflection. This process provides students with opportunities to recognize and capitalize on their own strengths and areas in need of improvement. As a result, they learn to set realistic goals for future endeavors. (See page 13.)

Rubric: This assessment tool includes a set of criteria used to determine the extent of the learning or the effectiveness and appearance of a product or accomplishment. They can be teacher-made or developed collaboratively with students. To increase the effectiveness of rubrics, remember to share them prior to the learning experience so students are thoroughly familiar with the criteria for an excellent performance. (See page 14.)

Peer evaluation: Discussing the criteria of a quality product with students prior to the peer evaluation is important. (You may want to provide and review a rubric or checklist.) Once they are more familiar with what to look for, students can critique their classmates during the process (to offer feedback that will contribute to the effectiveness of the final product) or after the project has been finished (following an oral presentation, for example).

Assessment should be ongoing throughout any learning process and not something that is done "to" students after the learning is considered completed. Involving students in the assessment process itself, making them knowledgeable about the criteria to be effective learners, will enhance the learning and facilitate the production of quality projects.

Student _____ Date_____

Self-Evaluation

Evaluate how you did on your project by using the following terms:

4	**Awesome!** I went beyond what I had to do on the project.
3	**Good Job.** I fulfilled all the requirements.
2	**Fair.** I met many of the requirements, but I could have done better.
1	**Needs Improvement.** I did not meet the requirements of the project.

Circle the rating that best describes how you did. Explain why you earned that rating.

1. I prepared for the project and did the required research.
Explain.

4	3	2	1

_____

_____

2. The information is accurate, organized, and relevant to my topic.
Explain.

4	3	2	1

_____

_____

3. I used a variety of appropriate resources to get the information.
Explain.

4	3	2	1

_____

_____

4. My handwriting is neat and legible (if handwritten) or I typed
the text neatly. Explain.

4	3	2	1

_____

_____

5. I used correct spelling, punctuation, and capitalization. I also
varied sentence structure. Explain.

4	3	2	1

_____

_____

6. I was careful in creating my project and was creative and original.
Explain.

4	3	2	1

_____

_____

The thing I liked best about my project is

_____

If I could do this project over again, I would

_____

I learned the following things by doing this project:

_____

Student _____ Date_____

Assessment Rubric

| **4** Exemplary | **3** Good | **2** Fair | **1** Needs Improvement |

Person Evaluating Project: ☐ Self ☐ Classmate ☐ Teacher

Content

4 Insightful knowledge of topic. Evidence of thorough research using multiple sources. No informational errors or glaring omissions.

3 Accurate knowledge and understanding of topic. Evidence of adequate research using several sources. No major errors or omissions.

2 Adequate understanding and knowledge of topic. Some evidence of research with limited number of sources. Most information correct but some inaccuracies.

1 Poor knowledge of topic. Contains few facts. Little evidence of research. Information may be copied from a single source. Major informational errors and omissions.

Organization and Development of Ideas

4 Excellent development and organization of ideas and information. Supported by quality details and examples.

3 Good development of ideas and information. Supported by ample examples and details.

2 Adequate development and partial organization of ideas. Some examples and details.

1 Minimal addressing of topic. Few details and examples. Plan of organization lacking.

Craftsmanship and Creativity

4 Creative and original work. Excellent selection and use of materials. Constructed with great care. Neatness exceptional.

3 Original and attractive work. Good selection and use of materials. Constructed with care and is neat.

2 Somewhat attractive project. Adequate selection and use of materials. Constructed with minimal care. Somewhat neat.

1 Not particularly interesting or attractive project. Poor selection and use of materials. Constructed carelessly.

Following Directions

4 Consistently listens to and follows oral directions and explanations. Project assembled properly and correctly.

3 Listens and follows directions most of the time. Project assembled properly.

2 Listens and follows directions some of the time. Project assembled somewhat properly.

1 Pays little attention to directions. Project not well assembled.

Conventions

4 Consistently uses correct spelling, punctuation, capitalization, grammar, and varied sentence structure.

3 Contains few errors in mechanics. Good use of varied sentence structure.

2 Contains several errors in mechanics. Some varied sentence structure.

1 Contains many major errors in mechanics. Errors interfere with meaning. Little variation in sentence structure.

Project Sharing and Presentation

4 Excellent presentation. Communicates effectively with audience. Effective voice projection and body language. Able to answer questions.

3 Good presentation. Communicates well with audience. Voice projections and pacing sufficient. Able to answer many questions. Shows confidence in body language.

2 Fair presentation. Some awareness of audience. Voice too loud or soft. Fair pacing. Can answer some questions. Demonstrates some confidence.

1 Poor delivery and organization of presentation. Unable to answer most questions. Insecure in delivery of presentation.

Scores by Category

Total Score

Content		Following Directions	
Organization and Development of Ideas		Conventions	
Craftsmanship and Creativity		Presentation and Sharing	

① Origami Pamphlet

The beauty of this structure lies in the fact that it requires only one scissor cut and one folded down piece of paper to create a pamphlet that contains six pages plus a front and back cover. Once the pamphlet has been completed, it can easily be unfolded and photocopied to share.

Materials, per student

- 1 sheet of paper (8½" x 11" or 11" x 17")
- scissors

Directions

1. Fold the sheet of paper in half, using the hot dog fold.

2. Open flat, smoothing the paper.

3. Fold in half the other way, using the book fold.

4. Curl one open edge to the fold. Crease.

5. Flip over.

6. Curl the other edge to the fold. Crease. Turn your paper so that it is in the shape of a "W."

7. Cut the fold line in the middle of the "W" to the point where the folds meet. The cut will look like a monster mouth.

8. Fold back. Then open the "mouth" completely so that the paper takes on the shape of an open book.

9. Close the book.

The Iroquois as Gatherers, Hunters, and Farmers

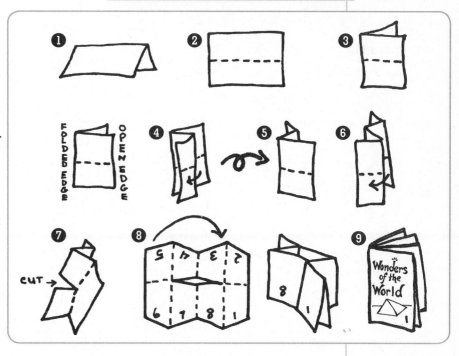

Project Idea

Facts About Philadelphia

When "visiting" Philadelphia, students can not only travel across the city visiting its museums, the Philadelphia Zoo, the Liberty Bell, and so on, but they can also travel back centuries to the colonial period of Benjamin Franklin.

Literature Connection

Kidding Around Philadelphia: A Young Person's Guide to the City
by Rebecca Clay (John Muir Publications, 1990)
Perfect kids' travel companion to the City of Brotherly Love.

Other Topic Ideas

• Facts About . . . (for example, Women During World War II, the Presidents)	• Famous Battles in the American Revolution (for example, Yorktown, Saratoga, Bunker Hill)
• World Monuments	• Cajun Life
• Native American Tools	• Occupations
• Three Branches of Government	• History of the American Flag

2 Side-by-Side Book

Variation: Side-by-Side Book With Origami Frame

To create this book, folded papers are glued together, side by side, so that students may create one spread of papers at a time. Therefore, students enjoy the freedom to continually add on more pages as the content increases. This structure lends itself to collaborative class projects, as works by different individuals or groups can be joined together easily.

Materials, per student

- 3 sheets of paper
  (cover weight, 8½" x 11")
- glue stick

Directions

1. Fold the three sheets of papers in half, one at a time, using the book fold.

2. Apply glue around the front edges of the second and third pieces of paper.

3. Glue papers together by laying one on top of the other.

4. Add more pages onto the end, as necessary.

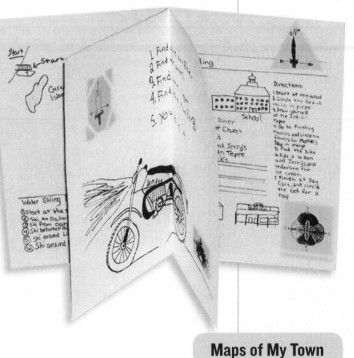

Maps of My Town

Variation: Side-by-Side Book With Origami Frame

By gluing origami frames into the side-by-side book, this format becomes a gallery of pictures. Students enjoy learning to fold paper to create a frame that enhances the project. (The sequence of folds is closely related in form to the popular, classic folding fortune-teller toy.)

Materials, per student

- 1 8½" paper square
- 1 piece of 3"-square drawing paper (or a suitable photo) to insert into frame
- Side-by-Side Book

Directions

1. Begin with an 8½" paper square.

2. Fold paper in half, then open flat.

3. Fold in half the other way and open again.

4. Fold corners to the middle.

5. Turn over the folded paper.

6. Fold corners to the middle.

7. Turn over the paper again.

8. Starting from the middle of the paper, fold the corner of each small square back toward its outside corner.

9. Insert picture into the frame by sliding the corners of the picture into the pockets of the frame. Decorate corners, if desired.

10. Glue frame into a page of a Side-by-Side Book, then repeat the steps to create frames for the other pages.

Liberty Framed

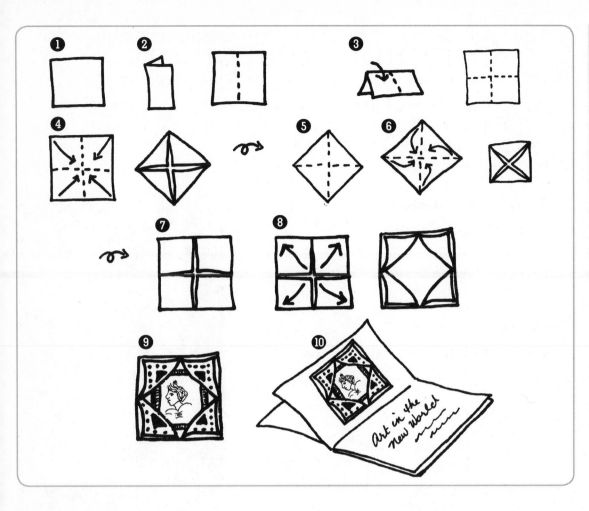

Project Idea

A View of the Medieval World

This book format is ideal to depict medieval life. If using the frames, students can display drawings of the outside of an ornate castle, its inhabitants, the clothing people wear, a scene from a feast, and so on.

Literature Connection

The Medieval World by Philip Steele (Kingfisher Publications, 2000)
Information about life in medieval times.

Other Topic Ideas

• World Landmarks	• Record Holders
• Explorers	• 21st-Century Inventions
• The Alamo	• People of India

③ Origami Caterpillar

Created from joined units of folded paper squares, this project unfolds with dynamic flourish. The length of it lends itself to timelines and charting out paths of exploration. Also, the folded sections can be utilized to define illustrated scenes, flanked by written information.

Materials, per student

- 3 8½" paper squares
- glue stick
- 2 4½" squares of cover weight paper (optional)

Directions

1. Fold each 8½" paper square paper in half.

2. Open flat. Fold in half the other way.

3. Open again and flip over.

4. Fold in half diagonally, open, and flip over.

5. Gently and completely, press down the center of the square.

6. Bring the points of the diagonal fold together, allowing the paper to form a smaller square.

7. Glue the squares together so the bottom of one small square slides into the top of the next small square.

8. Press down on the entire book carefully, making sure you don't create any new creases.

9. If desired, glue a square of cover weight paper onto the front and back cover for added sturdiness.

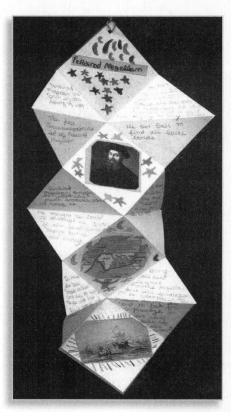

Explorers

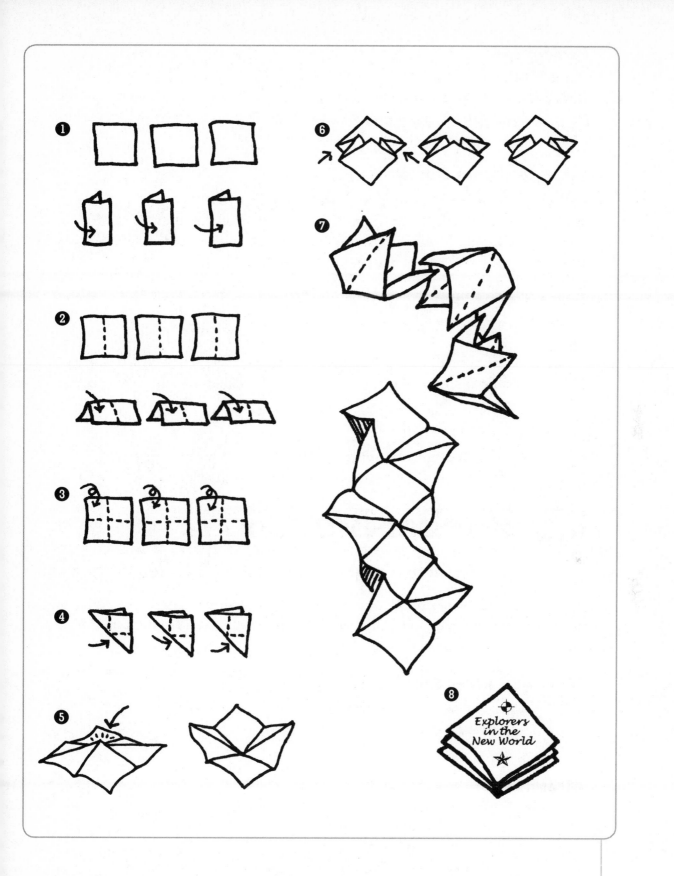

Explorers
in the
New World

Project Idea

Money, Money, Money

Have students choose a denomination of money, such as a dollar bill, a 50-cent piece, or state quarter, and tell about its journey—from its minting to traveling all over town, following the model of the suggested book.

Literature Connection

Follow the Money by Loreen Leedy (Holiday House, 2002)
Trace the journey of a quarter from first being stamped out at the U.S. Mint to traveling all around town: in a grocery store's cash register, soda machine, parking meter, and yard sale, before ending up in a bank.

Other Topic Ideas

• U.S. Monuments	• Sailing in America
• Journey Through China	• Life in a Colonial Village
• California Gold Rush	• Recycling a Can
• Biography (for example, presidents, athletes, writers, extraordinary women)	• From Farm to Table

4 Rubber-Band Book

Variation: Rubber-Band Book With Picture Corners

This simple structure is made from paper and a rubber band. The book can contain just a few or many pages. It works well for historically based journal entries, interesting facts, or short reports.

Materials, per student

- 2 sheets of paper, 8½" x 11"
- 1 #19 rubber band
- scissors

Directions

1. Fold two sheets of papers in half, one at a time, using the hot dog fold.

2. Cut along the fold to create four sheets of paper.

3. Fold each new sheet in half, bringing the short edges together.

4. Nest pages together.

5. Snip off corners from the top and bottom of the folded edge of the book.

6. Slide the rubber band onto the book so that it encircles the spine and the middle inside pages, thus snugly securing all the pages together.

Canadian Musicians

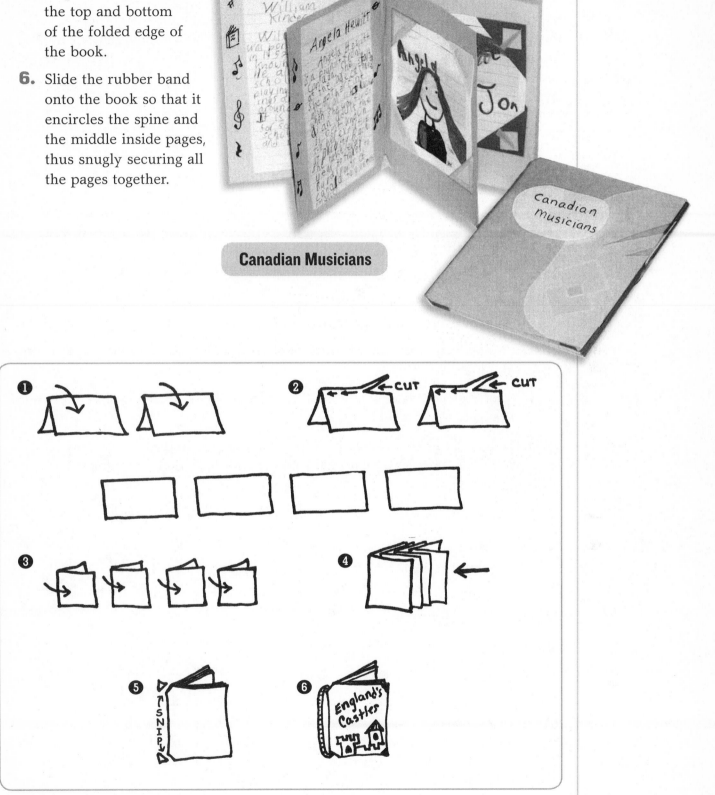

Variation: Rubber-Band Book With Picture Corners

Jazz up a simple Rubber-Band Book with student-created picture corners. Using these corners, students can insert (or easily change) photographs, charts, graphs, illustrations, and so on.

Materials, per student

- 4 small strips of paper, 1" x 3"
- glue stick
- drawing paper, 3½" x 3½"
- Rubber-Band Book

Directions

1. Begin with one small strip.

2. Perpendicularly fold down half of the strip.

3. Fold down the other half of the strip so that it meets the first fold (a point is created at the top).

4. Flip over to reveal a little corner pocket. (Slide this pocket onto the corner of a picture.)

5. Repeat steps 1–4 to create the three remaining corners and slide them onto the picture.

6. To attach the picture to a book page, apply glue to the corners only. This way, the picture can freely slide in and out of the little pockets.

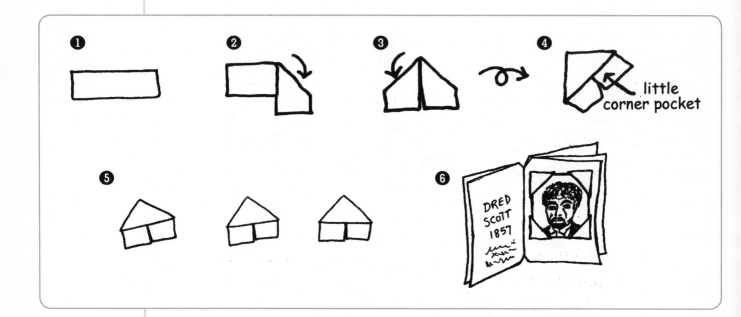

Tip!

To have a little more fun with the corners, try one of these ideas:

- Draw decorative shapes onto the corners.

- Snip off the tip of a corner to create a band.

- Nest two different colored corners together. Cut out shapes from the outer layer to show the inside color.

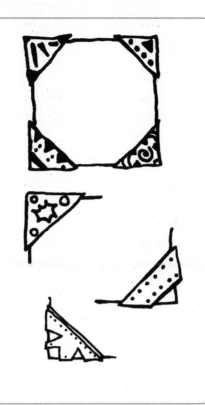

Project Idea

Kids in History

Students are always fascinated about the roles that young people played during a historic era. The Literature Connection suggested here describes young people who fought during the Civil War. Students could choose another period in history and create a Rubber-Band Book discussing such roles. They could also use this book as a journal or scrapbook, cutting out stories about how young people are making a difference in the world today.

Literature Connection

When Johnny Went Marching by Clifton Wisler (HarperCollins, 2001)
Stories of 49 young people who fought in the Civil War.

Other Topic Ideas

• Earth Day	• Traditions of the Sioux
• City Life	• Life in the Arctic
• Musical Eras or Genres	• 20th-Century Inventions

5 Belt Loop Logbook

This is a miniature book, worn as a necklace or hung from a belt loop. The fact that it is attached to a student makes it a good choice to use for short biographies or for note taking during field trips.

Materials, per student

- 4 strips of paper squares, 8½" x 2"
- 1 36" length of yarn
- 1 #16 rubber band
- beads (optional)

Directions

1. Begin with four strips of paper.

2. One at a time, fold each strip in half, using the book fold.

3. Nest folded strips together.

4. Cut away corners off the folded edge.

5. Double wrap the rubber band around the strips so that it encircles the middle, thus snugly securing the pages together.

6. Tie a piece of yarn to the rubber band.

7. If desired, decorate by stringing on some beads.

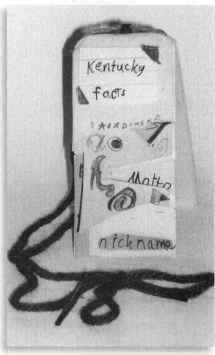

Kentucky Facts

Project Idea

Fun Facts

With this activity, students can wear fun and interesting facts or record-breaking information, which can be written as poems, as in *A Burst of Firsts*, or in a style similar to *The Guinness Book of World Records*.

Literature Connection

A Burst of Firsts by Patrick J. Lewis (Dial, 2001)
Poems about doers, shakers, and record-breakers.

Other Topic Ideas

• American Symbols	• Geographic Terms
• Important Rivers	• Statue of Liberty
• About My State (including landmarks, state flag, official flower, bird, and motto)	• Women of Valor (for example, Sacajawea, Clara Barton, Rosa Parks, Mother Teresa)
• Famous Athletes (for example, Michael Jordan, Derek Jeter, Serena Williams, Michelle Wie)	• Olympic Sports Through the Years

 Accordion Pockets

Made with a single piece of paper that folds to create a row of four pockets, this book creates pages with a holding pocket on each page. Students enjoy putting bits of gathered information, drawings, and notes in the separate pockets—and being able to move them, take them out to read, and replace them.

Materials, per student

- 1 sheet of paper, 8½" x 11"
- paper strips, about 5½" x 2"
- ribbon (optional)

Directions

1. Begin with one sheet of paper.

2. Fold in half, using the book fold.

3. Open flat.

Geography/Landforms

4. Create a pocket by folding up 2½" of the long edge.

5. Using the book fold, fold in half so that the pocket shows on the outside.

6. Fold one open edge over so that it is lined up to the middle fold.

7. Flip over.

8. Fold over the other edge so that it is lined up to the middle fold.

9. Secure the outside, open edges of the pockets with tape or staples.

10. If desired, to make a tie closure, put a hole at each edge, then run a long ribbon through the holes.

Have students collect information on paper strips and store them in the appropriate pockets. You may want to place a prompt on the part of the paper strips that is visible and have students use the lower part to fill in any information.

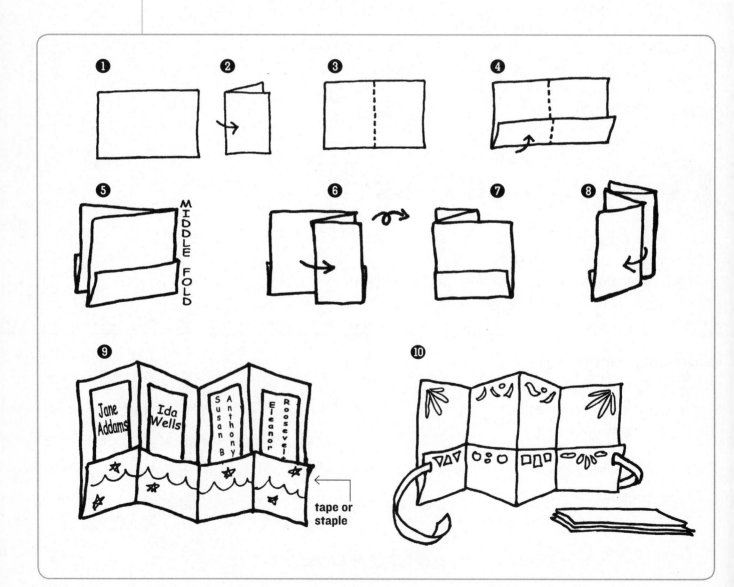

Project Idea

Bridges

Students can create a pocket book of bridges, choosing some from the book below or others they may discover in their research. For example, students might include the Brooklyn Bridge and the Golden Gate Bridge, as well as others in their own community. Encourage students to include illustrations or photographs and a history of the bridge, such as how it got its name.

Literature Connection

Bridges Are to Cross by Philemon Sturges (Putnam, 1998)
Features different types of bridges from Roman aqueducts, to the Tower Bridge in London, covered bridges, and more.

Other Topic Ideas

• Important Women in History	• Civil War Battles
• Sports Around the World	• Holidays
• Statistics About . . . (for example, athletes, world leaders, states)	• Documents or Speeches in American History
• My Timeline	• Natural Disasters

 # Butterfly Accordion

Variation: Butterfly Accordion With Paper Spring

This project is similar to the Side-by-Side Book, except that only the front outside edges of the papers are glued together. The advantage of this structure is how it opens, making it perfect for display.

Materials, per student

- 3 sheets of paper, 8½" x 11" (cover weight)
- glue stick

My Favorite Holiday

Directions

1. Fold the three sheets of papers in half, one at a time, using the book fold.

2. Apply a line of glue to the front outside edge of the second and third pieces of paper.

3. With the folded edges set next to each other, press edges together.

4. Add more pages onto the end of a finished Butterfly Accordion, as needed.

Variation: Butterfly Accordion With Paper Spring

Enhancing the project by adding a paper spring with a drawing attached to the end of it is fun and easy. The dynamic addition delightfully engages student interest.

Materials, per student

- 2 strips of paper, 8½" x 11"
- glue stick
- card weight drawing paper, about 3½" square
- Butterfly Accordion

Springing Around Liberty

Directions

1. Glue both strips together with the ends overlapping so that they form a right angle.

2. Start a pattern of carefully folding the lower strip over the strip on top.

3. Continue until a neat little square is formed. This square will expand into a spring.

4. Secure strip ends with a dab of glue.

5. Cut out a shape from the drawing paper and glue it to the top of the spring.

6. Glue the springing object onto a page of the Butterfly Accordion.

Project Idea

Countries of the World
Students can select a country and find out which products, crafts, foods, animals, sports, and so on are typical of that country. Encourage students to add the paper spring to some of the entries to give them a 3-D effect.

Literature Connection

Look What Came From Australia by Kevin Davis (Franklin Watts, 1999)
Describes many things that originally came from Australia, including inventions, sports, games, food, animals, words, and musical instruments.

Other Topic Ideas

• Presidential Snapshots	• State Quarters
• Easy Tips for Staying Safe	• Musical Instruments
• Ancient Egyptian Gods and Goddesses	• Inventors and Their Inventions

⑧ Wallet Book

The fully opened Wallet Book reveals three large pockets, which can also accommodate smaller books and projects.

Materials, per student

- 1 sheet of paper, 24" x 9" (cover weight)
- 3 sheets of paper, 8½" x 11"
- glue stick
- 1 36" length of ribbon, string, or yarn
- hand-held paper punch (available for all students to use)

Friendship

Directions

First prepare the three pockets.

1. One at a time, fold each sheet of paper in half, using the book fold.

2. Fold down a 2" flap from one of the open edges of each folded sheet.

3. Glue shut the sides of each pocket and set aside.

Continue by assembling the wallet.

4. Align the cover weight sheet vertically.

5. Glue one of the pockets about ¼" above the bottom edge of the sheet.

6. Create a fold in the cover sheet just above the top of this pocket.

7. Repeat steps 5 and 6 for the remaining two pockets to create three panels.

8. Fold down a 2" flap from the top of the outer corner.

9. Punch two holes through the double thickness of paper created by the flap.

10. Thread and secure ribbon through the holes. Fold the Wallet Book closed and tie ribbons around it to help keep it secure.

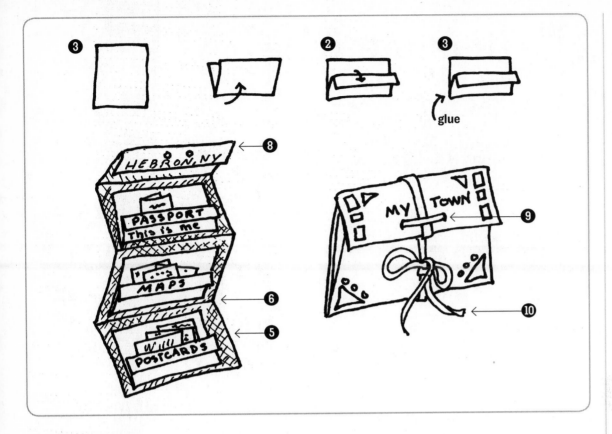

Project Idea

Aviation History
Students can devote each Wallet Book pocket to some aspect of aviation, such as female pilots, Orville and Wilbur Wright, modern planes, and airports of today.

Literature Connection

The Golden Age of Aviation by Katherine Williamson (Smithmark, 1996)
Covers the history of air travel from ancient times to modern day.

Other Topic Ideas

● Pioneer Life	● Let's Go Traveling to . . .
● Rural Life	● National Parks
● The Olympics	● Invented by Women

⑨ Timeline Tube

This project uses a cylinder and a rolled up scroll, which is inserted into the cylinder and then pulled through a slit to read frame by frame. The scroll, made from a long piece of paper or individual sheets taped together, can be laminated for durability and ease of handling. Use for timelines or any other sequencing activity.

Sports and Games Timeline

Materials, per student

- 1 cardboard cylindrical container (from packaging for oatmeal, drink mix, or potato chips, for example)
- roll of paper cut to size
- scissors
- adhesive paper or fabric
- glue stick

Directions

1. Cut a ¼"-wide slit in the container lengthwise (running almost the length, top to bottom).

2. Cover the container with adhesive paper, or glue fabric to the outside.

3. Cut a roll of paper to create a scroll that fits the height of the slit. (The length will vary according to how much space is needed for text and illustrations.)

4. Add information and drawings to the scroll.

5. Once the scroll is completed, roll it up. (Start rolling from the last bit of information first.)

6. Place the scroll inside the container.

7. Put the leading edge through the slit and continue pulling to reveal the text to read.

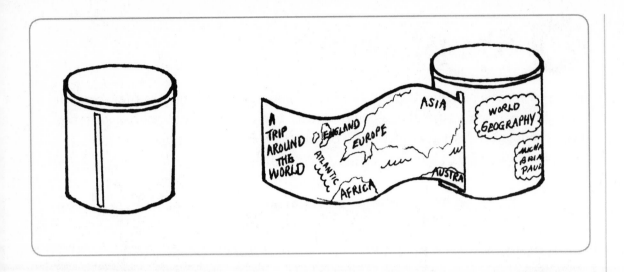

Project Idea

Life Story
Students use the timeline tube format to create a biography of a famous American. For example, have students each contribute a tube focusing on a key figure in the civil rights movement (Martin Luther King, Jr., Jackie Robinson, Shirley Chisholm, and so on).

Literature Connection

If a Bus Could Talk: The Story of Rosa Parks by Faith Ringgold
(Simon & Schuster, 1999)
Story of Rosa Parks, whose historic bus ride contributed to the civil rights movement.

Other Topic Ideas

• Journey Down the Mississippi	• How a Bill Becomes a Law
• The Mummification Process	• Order of Statehood
• From Raw Material to Finished Product	• Events Leading to the American Revolution

Shape Book

Shape Books take on the shape or outline of something that typifies their content. For example, a book on shelters could appear as a castle or house shape. A report about the logging industry could be written in a tree-shaped book.

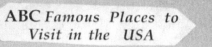

ABC: Famous Places to Visit in the USA

Materials, per student

- 2 sheets of oaktag for front and back covers
- several sheets of 8½" x 11" plain or lined paper
- binding materials (brad fasteners, staples, or spiral binding)
- scissors

Directions

Note: For binding purposes, consider these important points:

- Keep one side—either the top or the left edge—straight.

- Be sure front and back covers are slightly larger than the pages that will be used for the text and illustrations inside the book.

1. For the front cover, draw an outline on a piece of oaktag that best represents the shape of the topic.

2. Cut out the shape, taking care to leave one area straight to allow for the binding.

3. For the back cover, again use a piece of oaktag. If desired, trace the shape of the front cover onto the other piece of oaktag. Cut out the shape.

4. Gather the paper for the inside pages. Use them as is, cut them to reflect the basic shape of the cover (rectangular, square, or triangular), or mimic the precise shape of the cover itself.

5. Bind together the cover and inside pages.

Project Idea

Eating Around the World
Following the model of the book below, have students write about the history of cooking and eating utensils, food habits, and manners. Possibilities for a book shape include a hand, cooking pot, or food item.

Literature Connection

What You Never Knew About Fingers, Forks, and Chopsticks
by Patricia Lauber (Simon & Schuster, 1999)
Beginning with the Stone Age, read about the history of cooking and eating utensils, dietary habits, and manners.

Other Topic Ideas

• Artist Biography	• All About Money
• Modes of Transportation	• Shelter
• Places (states, countries, continents)	• World-Famous Landmarks

11 Graduated-Pages Book

Variation: Shaped Graduated-Pages Book

Similar to dictionaries or directories that provide easy access to the inside contents through tools on the edges of pages, this project contains pages that are folded in such a way that leaves the edge of each one showing when it's closed. Graduated-Pages Books are especially suitable when an author wants to display key words, specific topics, and so on, that are readily visible to readers.

Materials, per student

- several sheets of 8½" x 11" construction paper
- binding materials (brad fasteners, staples, or spiral binding)
- colorful labels, paint chips, or contrasting paper
- glue stick
- scissors (optional)

Directions

State History

1. Fold or cut the leading edge of each page so that it overlaps with a small piece of paper showing on each page in succession.

2. The result is a book in which each successive page is slightly wider (if bound on the left) or longer (if bound on the top).

3. Once the pages are aligned satisfactorily, bind to make the book more secure.

4. Use the narrow strips that are visible to write labels, or glue on paint chips to create thumb tab indexes.

Variation: Shaped Graduated-Pages Book

Similar to the Shape Book, this book can also take on a shape that reflects the contents, in addition to aligning the pages so that the contents are visible on the edges. Follow the steps above. Then use scissors to cut out the chosen shape. Try individual state shapes for a state study, castles for medieval study, trees for information on rain forests, or houses for a study on shelters.

Project Idea

Ancient Egypt

This topic works well with either of the formats above. Students relay information about ancient Egypt. Each page can discuss some aspect of ancient Egyptian life, such as the pharaohs, mummification process, and hieroglyphics.

Ancient Egypt

Literature Connection

Ancient Egypt Revealed by Peter Chrisp, Sue Davidson, Ben Morgan (DK Publishing, 2002)
Explains how pyramids were built, how pharaohs were prepared for burials, and how to read hieroglyphs. Uses some transparent overlay pages.

Other Topic Ideas

• Penny History	• History of Stamps
• Space Exploration	• Colonial Life
• Great Adventurers (for example, Daniel Boone, Lewis and Clark, Sir Francis Drake)	• Biography (for example, world leaders, Nobel Prize winners, artists)

12 Fold-Out Book

A piece of mural paper or another extra-long sheet of paper works best with this project. After construction, the result is similar to a double-sided brochure. The format lends itself well to linear material, such as timelines, sequential development, biographical information, and so on.

Materials, per student

- 1 strip of mural paper, 8" x 24"
- ruler

Directions

1. Measure to find the center of the paper.

2. Make an erasable pencil mark at the top and bottom of the center.

3. Take the left edge of the paper and, holding it up, push the middle of it toward the pencil mark, keeping the edge still on the left. The paper must make a curl inward and outward like a backward "S."

4. Adjust the middle of curl so that it will align with the center mark on the paper and its edge will align on the left once the paper is pressed down and creased.

5. Repeat these steps for the right side.

6. Crease both sides again so that the book will lie flat when closed.

7. To open, pull the two top pieces outward.

The History of the United States

Project Idea

Our Nation's Capital
Create a fold-out map of Washington, D.C., our nation's capital. Students can include important buildings, monuments, and historical information.

Literature Connection

Capitol by Lynn Curlee (Atheneum, 2003)
Describes the buildings and monuments of Washington, D.C.

Other Topic Ideas

• Fold-Out Maps	• Age of Exploration
• The Oregon Trail	• Flags From Around the World
• Describe and Illustrate Historic Documents (for example, Preamble to the Constitution, the Gettysburg Address, the Pledge of Allegiance)	• Behind the Scenes (for example, of a historical event)

13 Plastic-Bag Book

Using see-through resealable plastic bags, with each one serving as an individual page, this book provides protective coverings for photos, pastels, or any other materials (such as leaves or fabric) that may be difficult to use.
Try to provide the bag size most suitable to a project.
Quart or gallon sizes generally work the best. Bags can ultimately be bound like a book or taped together as a display "quilt."

7 Regions of New York State

Materials, per student

- 6–8 resealable plastic bags (which provides 12–16 pages for writing, illustrating, and inserting photographs or other materials)
- tagboard
- vinyl tape
- scissors

Directions

1. Insert a piece of tagboard, cut to size, into each plastic bag.

2. Place the first bag on a clean surface, such as a desktop.

3. Use the bottom edge of the bag for binding.

4. Cut a piece of wide vinyl tape the exact length of the edge of the bag.

5. Carefully place the tape along the binding edge, with half of the tape on the bag itself and the other half stuck to the desk.

6. Place the second bag directly on top of the first bag and place another piece of tape exactly over the first piece.

individual plastic bags,
opening end facing out

7. Repeat this process for each of the bags.

8. After all the bags are taped together, lift the entire stack and carefully fold the exposed half of the tape over. The folded stack of tape strips will create the spine.

9. Now sheets of paper, photos, and so on, can be inserted or removed on either side of the tagboard still in the plastic sleeves.

Project Idea

Places in Postcards

Students create their own postcard books (using the book below as a model). They choose any destination that appeals to them or one you assign from class. Encourage students to correspond with people from other places using postcards, or they can create their own postcards, featuring information that is pertinent or fascinating about the area.

Literature Connection

Postcards From China by Zoe Dawson (Steck Vaughn, 1996)
Information about China presented in a postcard format.

Other Topic Ideas

• The Chocolate Journey	• Famous Waterways
• If You Were There . . . (for example, aboard the *Mayflower*, at Valley Forge in winter, at George Washington's inauguration)	• A Visit to . . . (for example, ancient Greece, Idaho, the Great Lakes, the Alps)

14 Facts-and-Figures Brochure

Capitalize on the interest in travel brochures to give students a realistic and meaningful context of doing their research. Their classmates will find reading the Facts-and-Figures Brochures informative and interesting.

Ancient Civilizations

Materials, per student

- 1 large piece of construction paper or tagboard
- ruler

Directions

1. Orient the paper horizontally.

2. Measure to find the center of the paper.

3. Make an erasable pencil mark at the top and bottom of the center.

4. Fold the left edge to the center and crease the fold.

5. Fold the right edge to the center and crease the fold. If desired, flip over and fold in half to look like a traditional brochure.

6. To open, lift each folded piece outward.

(fold back here, optional)

Project Idea

Agriculture

Students can explore agriculture and its role in our society, then create brochures about farms and farming.

Literature Connection

Farm by Ned Halley (Dorling Kindersley, 2000)
A close-up look at the history of farming from the first farms, the important role of animals and machinery, the variety of farms, and the future of farming.

Other Topic Ideas

• Industrial Revolution	• Art Around the World
• Winter Celebrations	• Schools: Long Ago and Today
• Ancient Cultures (for example, Aztecs, Mayas, Incas)	• Let's Visit . . . (for example, Kenya, Iceland, India, Argentina)
• A Day at the Museum	• Erie Canal

15 Envelope Book

This unique book binds several envelopes together along the left edges using key ring, spiral binding, or ribbons tied through punched holes. The "pages," or individual envelopes, can hold several pieces of information, artifacts, photographs, and so on. The outside of each envelope can be decorated and labeled to reflect the contents. This book is ideal for collecting information over a period of time since information can be added whenever it is identified. The size of Envelope Books varies according to the envelopes you select.

Materials, per student

- tagboard
- several envelopes, 1 for each page (any size, but the size of all envelopes within a single book should match)
- paper cut to match envelope size (optional)
- binding materials (brad fasteners, staples, yarn, ribbon, or spiral binding)
- index cards

The Life and Times of Benjamin Franklin

Directions

1. Cut two pieces of tagboard the size of the envelopes being used as pages. These will serve as the front and back covers.

2. Punch holes along the left edge of each envelope and the tagboard for binding.

3. If using regular paper between the envelopes for including additional text or illustrations, punch a hole in each of those sheets that will align with the holes in the tag board and envelopes.

4. Label the envelopes.

5. Decorate, as desired.

6. Record information on the index cards and insert them into the envelopes.

Project Idea

Explorers

Each envelope page in a book about explorers could hold a biographical summary, maps, and a timeline for each person included in the book. Perhaps have students focus on space explorers and research NASA astronauts.

Literature Connection

The Usborne Book of Explorers From Columbus to Armstrong by Felicity Everett and Struan Reid (Usborne Publishing, 1991)
Features information about how exploration and discoveries have changed our world.

Other Topic Ideas

• USA—State by State	• Local Community
• South America	• Money
• 13 Colonies	• Twentieth Century by Decade

16 Folded-Circle Book

The fun of this book is its shape. Circular sheets are folded into quarters and cut in such a way that these quarters become the pages. Unlike traditional books where pages turn over one another, to read this book, the pages are folded over and over in an interesting way.

Materials, per student

- 2 or more sheets of copy or construction paper
- scissors
- compass or other circular template (optional)

Directions

1. Cut out two identical large circles.

2. Fold each circle into quarters.

3. Crease them and then unfold.

4. Cut the radius of one circle and place it on the other circle with the slit at the top.

Symbols of America

5. The upper right-hand quarter will fold down to cover the lower right, exposing page 1 of the book. Write text on page 1 and illustrate on page 2 (the turned-down quarter now visible under page 1).

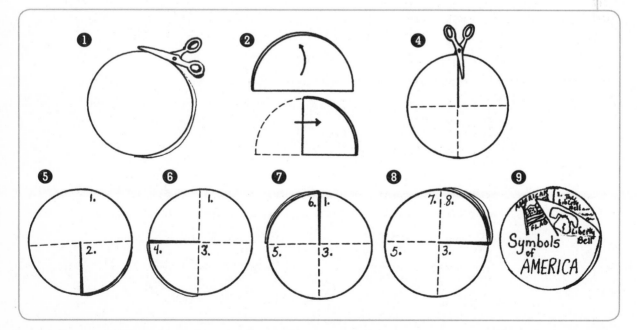

6. Fold two pieces to the left to expose the next set of pages. Write text on page 3 and illustrate on page 4 (to the left of page 3).

7. Fold three pieces upward to expose page 5, for writing, and page 6 above it, for illustrating.

8. Finally, fold the four pieces at the taped point to create the final page and illustration (pages 7 and 8).

9. Decorate the cover with a title, author name, and an illustration.

Project Idea

Facts About the Middle Ages
Students show pictures and facts about the Middle Ages on alternating pages.

Literature Connection

How Would You Survive in the Middle Ages? by Fiona MacDonald
(Franklin Watts, 1995)
Transports the reader back in time to the Middle Ages, giving information on the aspects of daily life in medieval times.

Other Topic Ideas

• Famous Aviators	• Women's Role in the Civil War
• How to Make . . . (for example a law, paper, a log home)	• History of . . . (for example, Michigan, the Underground Railroad, the Battle of Saratoga)
• Historical Fiction (retell or write)	• Hemisphere Study

Slit Book

When other materials aren't readily available, this is the perfect book! It requires only a few sheets of paper. The way the paper is cut along the spine, when folded, allows the sheets to slip into place and remain together as a book. This simple book is a favorite with students. It's also great for taking notes.

Materials, per student

- several sheets of copy, construction, or lined paper, 8½" x 11"
- scissors

Directions

1. Fold several sheets of paper in half, using the book fold.

2. Take one of those sheets and cut a slit along the fold's center. Be sure to leave the top and the bottom of the fold uncut, about 1 inch from each edge.

3. On the rest of the sheets, cut a slit a little longer than 1 inch from the top and the bottom edges, along the center of the fold.

4. Roll this group of sheets together, perpendicular to the fold. Slide the roll into the slit of the first sheet.

5. When the center of the roll meets the center of the single sheet, let it unroll.

6. Flatten the pages so the edge slits will fall on each side of the single sheet's center.

7. Crease all the sheets along the original center fold lines to complete the book and help it stay together.

Women Who Made a Difference in American History

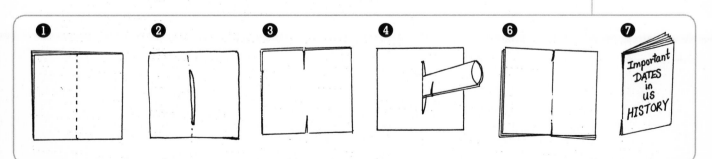

Project Idea

Presidential Facts

Students learn interesting tidbits about life and living in the White House. Students can include interesting facts about the presidents and their families to write their version. This book could also serve as a model for portraying other famous buildings or locations, such as the Alamo or Plimoth Plantation.

Literature Connection

Ghosts of the White House by Cheryl Harness (Simon & Schuster, 1998)
A guided fictional tour of the White House where presidential "ghosts" offer intriguing tidbits from their presidential years.

Other Topic Ideas

• Parts of a Map	• Life on an Island
• History of Transportation	• Money From Around the World
• Ancient Roman Gods and Goddesses	• California Missions

⑱ Matchbook Report

Inspired by an old-fashioned book of paper matches, the fold-over top of this project protects its inner pages and although it can be made in any size, students may find the smaller ones more appealing because they are very portable.

Materials, per student

- 1 small piece of oaktag
- several small pieces of plain or lined paper
- scissors
- stapler

Directions

1. Cut the piece of oaktag to form a long, narrow rectangle.

2. Use this piece to create the front and back covers for the project. Fold it lengthwise, leaving a half-inch piece extending beyond one edge.

3. Fold this half-inch piece over the top of the main part of the project. (This small flap creates the lip where the inner sheets will be stapled.)

4. Cut several sheets of paper (plain or lined) to fit into the small flap. Staple them near the crease.

5. Tuck the top fold into the flap to create the cover.

6. As necessary, slightly trim the top corner piece to clear the staples.

Facts About American Wars

Project Idea

Patriotic Symbols

Students can create a collection featuring some of our country's patriotic symbols. A small illustration with a caption is all that's needed for the symbols in this "proud to be an American" tribute.

Literature Connection

Read, White, Blue, and Uncle Who? by Teresa Bateman (Holiday, 2001)
The story behind some of America's patriotic symbols.

Other Topic Ideas

• World Records	• Inspiring or Famous Quotes
• Civic Holidays	• Oceans of the World
• Facts About . . . (for example, the Olympics, the Civil War, Landforms)	• Volcanic Eruptions

19 Artifact-Bound Book

What makes this format unique is the binding. These books are bound using an object that symbolizes the contents of the book, rather than stapling or sewing the binding. For example, a twig might bind a book about trees and the logging industry, a spoon might bind a recipe book focusing on a specific period of history, or a paintbrush might bind a book about art in history. This project can really be any size. The length of the bound edge will be determined by the length of the object to be used.

Materials, per student

- tagboard
- plain or lined paper
- object for binding (for example, straw, stick, spoon, feather, pencil)
- rubber band
- yarn, string, twin, or ribbon (optional)

Directions

1. To use tagboard for the front and back covers, punch two holes along the left or top edge. This divides the edge into thirds. (For larger books, use three holes.)

2. Use a rubber band to hold the binding object in place. Hold the rubber band under the back cover. Push one end of the rubber band up through one hole, creating a small loop.

3. Place the end of the object through the loop.

4. Pull down on the band to tighten it.

5. Extend the other end of the rubber band up through the second hole.

6. Insert the object through the loop to secure the binding. Make sure the rubber band fits snugly (but not so tight it will break).

7. As needed, you may also use yarn, string, twine, or ribbon to secure the binding object.

History of the U.S. Flag

Project Idea

Japanese Culture

Students research and write about aspects of Japanese culture. To bind their finished project, they may want to use a chopstick or a calligraphy brush.

Literature Connection

Japan by Ena Keo (Steck Vaughn, 1998)
An informational book about Japan.

Other Topic Ideas

• Baseball Greats	• Hawaii: The Aloha State
• Unusual Occupations	• Recipes From Pilgrim Times
• My Town: Past and Present	• Recipes From Around the World

20 Biography Hanger

Open up your closets and retrieve wire hangers to create people-like figures that can hang or stand up by themselves. Left in original hanger shape, they can be hung on hooks in the classroom or tacked to bulletin boards. For the stand-up version, simply fold in the two "arms" of the hanger and you have created figures that can sit on windowsills, students' desks, or in a showcase.

Materials, per student

- wire hanger (thin ones work best)
- large piece of construction paper or oaktag (18" x 24")
- heavy-duty tape
- scissors
- plain or lined paper

Directions

1. Center a hanger on the large piece of construction paper. Be sure the hook extends over the top edge.

2. Fold the paper along the angle to cover the "shoulder" wires.

3. Use tape to secure the paper.

4. Turn the covered hanger over. (This piece represents an upper torso.)

Amelia Earhart was an American pilot. She was born in Kansas in 1897. She is most famous for being the first woman to fly all by herself across the Atlantic Ocean in 1932. Just five years later, she disappeared during her last flight.

Amelia Earhart

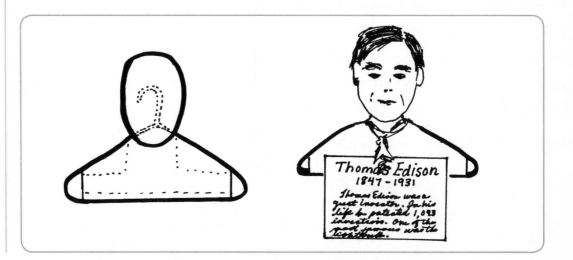

Thomas Edison
1847 - 1931

Thomas Edison was a great inventor. In his life he patented 1,093 inventions. One of the most famous was the lightbulb.

5. Cut out a circle or oval about 4 or 5 inches in diameter.

6. Tape the circle onto top of the hanger. (This piece represents a head.)

7. Decorate, or "dress," the pieces to resemble a person.

Project Idea

Lewis and Clark

Inspired by the Literature Connection book below, students create a hanger of explorers Lewis or Clark based on the point of view of the Newfoundland dog that was part of their famous journey. Students can write on plain or lined paper and tape it to the front of the explorer's torso.

Literature Connection

Lewis and Clark and Me: A Dog's Tale by Laurie Meyers (Scholastic, 2001) The famous expedition of Lewis and Clark told from their dog's perspective.

Other Topic Ideas

• U.S. Presidents	• Kids Who Made a Difference
• Characters in Historical Fiction	• Hall of Heroes
• Traditional Dress Around the World	• World Leaders

21 Pocket-Folder Book

This simply made book opens to present two pairs of staggered pockets. Students gather information onto filing cards, which they then place in the appropriately labeled pockets.

Famous Kentuckians

Materials, per student

- 2 sheets of paper, 8½" x 11"
- filing cards

Directions

1. Begin with one sheet of paper.

2. Fold in half, using the book fold.

3. Open flat.

4. Create a pocket by folding up 2½" of the long edge.

5. Cut away a tiny triangle from the bottom center. Set aside.

6. Fold the second sheet of paper in half, using the book fold.

7. Open flat.

8. Fold in half, using the hot dog fold.

9. With its folded edge up, slip this piece into the pocket of the first piece of paper.

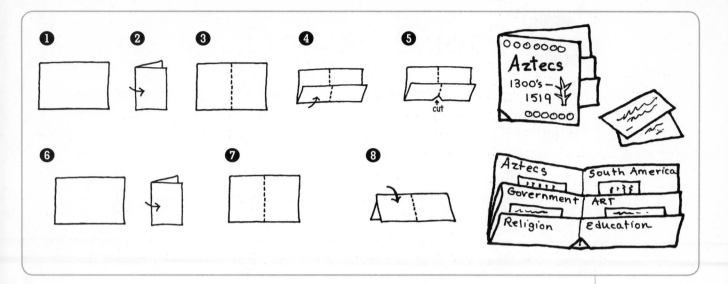

10. To finish the project, label the top edges with the research topic, label the pockets with any research categories, and collect information on filing cards, storing them in the appropriate pockets.

11. If desired, secure the outside, open edges of the pockets with tape or staples. To make a tie closure, put a hole at each edge, then run a long ribbon through the holes.

Project Idea

Daily Activities of Children in History
To feature the daily activities of children in the 19th century, for example, students can include many types of categories, such as toys, dinner time, going to school, doing chores, and county fairs.

Literature Connection

Historic Communities: A Child's Day by Bobbie Kalman (Crabtree, 1994)
A glimpse into the day-to-day life of children in 19th-century North American communities.

Other Topic Ideas

• States and Capitals	• Favorite State or National Parks
• A Look at Ancient Rome	• Types of Maps
• Celebrations Around the World	• White House
• A Visit to . . . (for example, New Zealand, Antarctica, the Nile River, the Grand Canyon)	• Political Parties (Through the Years)

22 Topic Box

This kind of "book" is a collection of objects, artifacts, and writings placed in decorated boxes. All of the contents relate to a specific topic or theme. The outside of the box is generally decorated and includes the kind of information that is found on the cover of a book.

Penny Research

Materials, per student

- a sturdy shoe or boot box (any size)
- paint or adhesive paper
- index card or colored tagboard
- scissors

Other Container Options

• paper grocery bag	• leftover gift bag
• lunch boxes	• small suitcases
• boxes with see-through lids	• briefcases

Directions

1. Select a box or other container.

2. Decorate the box, using paint or adhesive paper.

3. Decorate a card that includes a title and author for the Topic Box.

4. Collect items to place in the box that support the topic or theme.

5. Write an explanation for why each item is included.

Project Idea

State Study

Students place objects that represent a state in their decorated box. For example, objects representing Massachusetts might include lobsters, cranberries, beach sand, a postcard of Boston, a brochure from Plimoth Plantation, a state map, and pictures or newspaper articles.

Literature Connection

M Is for Mayflower: A Massachusetts Alphabet by Margot Raven
(Sleeping Bear Press, 2002)
Presents information about the Commonwealth of Massachusetts in an alphabetical arrangement.

Other Topic Ideas

• Abraham Lincoln	• Community Changes Over Time
• Life in a Colonial Seaport	• Life in a Frontier Town
• Sports Heroes	• Follow an Election

23 File-Folder Book

Create a book using a simple file folder. The front of the folder acts as a traditional cover, with a title, author, and illustration. Inside is perfect for a variety of information on any topic.

Materials, per student

- file folder (standard or legal)
- tagboard, library card pockets, or envelopes
- glue stick
- tape
- index cards
- scissors

Directions

1. Decorate the front of a file folder with title and author information. Add an illustration, if desired.

2. Glue envelopes inside the folder to create pockets to store information. Or, cut tagboard into shapes and tape them to the inside of the folder.

3. While researching a topic, write information on index cards and add them to the appropriate pocket. (Be sure to label the pockets to make retrieving information later easier.)

The Mary Celeste

Project Idea

History Mystery

Students research a mysterious event in history and create a book that includes their own predictions as to what happened. Possible topics include the *Mary Celeste*, Amelia Earhart's disappearance, or the Lost Colony of Roanoke.

Literature Connection

The Mary Celeste: An Unsolved Mystery From History by Jane Yolen and Heidi Yolen Stemple (Simon & Schuster, 2001)

Relates the tale of the unexplained disappearance of the crew on the ship *Mary Celeste* in 1872 and challenges readers to solve the mystery.

Other Topic Ideas

• Polar Regions	• Gulf of Mexico
• Navajo Code-Talkers	• The Great Lakes
• Where in the World Am I?	• U.S. Neighbors: Canada and Mexico

24 3-D Snapshot

Similar to a diorama that is made in a shoe box, this project uses three sheets of paper or tagboard to create the illusion of depth. Students can develop their ability to use perspective drawing and scale to make the scenes more realistic. These 3-D Snapshots make a great addition to windowsills, library shelves, and display cases.

Materials, per student

- 1 sheet of tagboard or heavy paper
- scissors
- stapler

Directions

1. Cut a sheet of paper into three strips of equal width.

2. Then cut one strip three inches shorter in length and another strip two inches shorter.

3. Before assembling the three pieces together, add illustrations and any writing.

4. Use the longest piece to draw the background (such as mountains, clouds, and distant views).

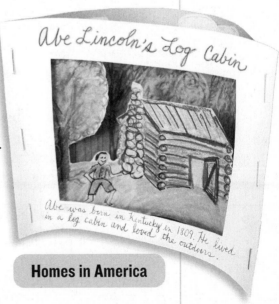

Abe Lincoln's Log Cabin

Abe was born in Kentucky in 1809. He lived in a log cabin and loved the outdoors.

Homes in America

5. Use the medium strip for drawing main objects (such as historical buildings and monuments). Cut around the tops of these objects so the background will appear once the project is assembled.

6. Use the shortest piece for the front of the book. Cut out the center of this piece so it appears as a frame. Also add writing to this piece.

7. To assemble, place the shortest piece in the front, the medium piece in the middle, and the longest piece in the back. Align the edges and staple. The front piece should appear straight across and the other two pieces should curve slightly to help the project stand up on its own.

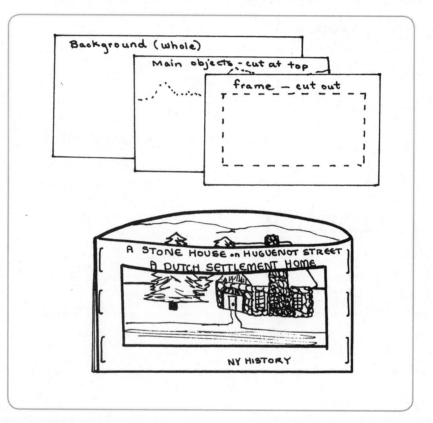

Project Idea

Key Events of the American Revolution

Students recreate key events of the American Revolution. For example, an illustration of the Boston Tea Party could have colonists on the docks on the middle layer, with the ships in the harbor drawn on the background piece.

Literature Connection

The American Revolution for Kids by Janis Herbert (Chicago Review Press, 2002) Detailed history book, covering American history from the Stamp Act and the Boston Tea Party to the British surrender at Yorktown and the creation of the U.S. Constitution.

Other Topic Ideas

• Famous Canals	• 19th-Century Inventions
• Lighthouses	• On the Job
• Presidential Childhood Homes	• Mountain Ranges

(25) Stick Book

A variation on the colonial Horn Book, Stick Books are generally single-paged books made from cardboard or paper with a stick handle. They are similar to posters or placards and can have information or visuals on the front and back.

Materials, per student

- heavy paper or tagboard
- tongue depressor or similar stick
- glue stick

Directions

1. Fold a piece of tagboard or heavy paper in an interesting way. For example, try an accordion fold, gathered at the bottom, to create a fan.

2. Decorate the front and back panels. (Use ideas based on other projects created earlier.)

3. Attach the paper to the wooden stick.

I'm a Fan of New York State

Project Idea

What Is America?

Students can each create a different aspect of America, from geography, to place, to people. If possible, represent different areas of the country and affix the finished projects to a map of the United States, placing them in their appropriate spots.

Literature Connection

America Is . . . by Louise Borden (Simon & Schuster, 2002)
Poetic text provides highlights about many aspects of our country and American lifestyles, such as farmland, prairies, cities, beaches, famous Americans, and the variety and diversity of the nation.

Other Topic Ideas

• Advertisements for Historical Events (or Artifacts)	• Games and Toys in a Historical Era
• Elections and Voting	• America A–Z
• History of Flight	• Civil Rights
• Ancient Greek Gods and Goddesses	• State Nicknames